You Got This!

A Girl's Guide To Growing Up

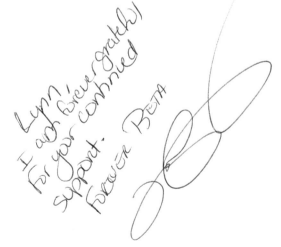

Lynn Brever grateful
I am grateful
For your continued
support.
Forever Beth

DR. TYFFANI MONFORD DENT

ISBN: 1500908878
ISBN 13: 9781500908874

dedication

For Tylar

& as always

Lynn, who *knew* but never got the chance to see

acknowledgements

To the Delta Academy Girls of Queens Alumnae Chapter
and Lima CTAG-Girls Program for their input.
You made this a much better book

Marcie Thomas of Brown Girl Collective
for providing the foreword

Kenya K. Taylor for taking on the hard task of editing,
just because I asked……

Monique Brown and Sherita Carthon for the
cover idea and design

Dr. Satira Streeter and Charita Selden for their input on
certain topic areas. Your experience in working with girls
provided much-needed recommendations

Becky Palmer and Jennifer Grooms for feedback

Carolyn Strong for valuable insight into bullying

Sonia Jackson Myles of The Sister Accord, LLC

All of the women who offered words of encouragement
to the next generation of women

Angel Cowan & Angela Warren (CTAG) and
Selvena Brooks & Kishshana Palmer (Delta Academy) for
allowing me to invade your programs just by saying
"I have this idea for a teen workbook…."

Travis Dent who continues to support me in all I do

My daughters who patiently allow Mommy time to write

Tyffani Dent
Summer 2014

foreword

I come to you as a former teenager who did a lot of things right; however, I also made my own fair share of mistakes during the most critical years of my life. You may not think that adults truly understand the things that you deal with on a daily basis. Girl, trust me, we know all too well. Yet, I recognize that a lot of things were much easier for those of us who grew up in generations past.

As I read through this book, Dr. Tyffani's words struck a chord for me as I recalled dealing with my parents' divorce. In a 4-year period of my life, I was trying to make friends in three different high schools. There I was attempting to understand boys and sexuality, figuring out what I wanted to be when I grew up, and struggling to determine who I wanted to be in this world. How I wish that I would have had a book like this one to assist me in making better choices during that season of my life!

The social media culture in which we live today is probably the most significant and impactful factor that separates the experiences from my own youth and those that you encounter today. Social media is a tool that allows us to learn about different people from all around the world. \Unfortunately, it also provides individuals the means to rapidly spread negativity. In as little as 10 seconds, an individual can take the most private of situations and expose it to the world. This book will also help educate you on how to manage your space in the online arena.

One of the most challenging times of any young woman's life lies in the years that she makes the transition from a little girl into a woman. Faced with internal emotional and physical changes, in addition to the pressures and expectations that come from the outside, the path towards adulthood is not always an easy one.

I created Brown Girl Collective a few years ago with the intention of developing something that would help girls (and adult women) celebrate their boldness, brilliance and beauty. It is that platform that led me to discover Dr. Tyffani. We have developed a strong partnership because she is equally committed to helping females to discover their own power---one good decision at a time. She is not only an outstanding professional, but a dedicated mother of two girls who wants the best for ALL girls, not just her own, and that passion shines through in her work.

The book that you hold in your hands is here to serve as a guide to help you navigate the path towards adulthood and help you to turn the crooked roads straight. My hope is that you will utilize the wisdom that is contained within as a GPS system to lead and direct you towards greatness. Turn the page and get started. You've got this!

Marcie L. Thomas
Founder/Chief Creative Officer
Brown Girl Collective

choices

Sometimes, it appears that there is only one choice to make when we encounter certain situations; however; in every situation, you have at least two choices. You either do something or you don't. Sounds pretty simple right?

Our lives are made up of decisions that need to be made almost every second of every day. Take a minute to write down every choice you had to make from the moment you woke up this morning (that was one choice----to stay in bed or get up) to right at this very moment when you are reading this.

the choices i have made today

1. _____

2. _____

3. _____

4. _____

5. _____

choices

Do you see how you are constantly making choices every moment of every day in your life? The problem with choices is that they do not just affect you *just* in that moment. Your choices can affect you far in to your future. It is extremely important that when you are making a choice that you consider *all* of the potential positive and negative effects your choice will have. Don't just sit and think about the immediate impact of your decision. Ask yourself, "If I do this, how can it affect my future?"

As young ladies, it can be difficult to think about becoming an adult It is hard, and not real exciting, to consider how your decisions will impact you when you are older. Often, there is so much going on in your life that to focus so far into the future can be quite a stretch.

It might even be difficult for you to look at the past choices that you have made. You might have made a few bad or embarrassing ones during your lifetime. No one likes to remember the bad choices or mistakes they have made. Many times, reflecting on our bad choices can cause us to feel:

1. Angry

2. Sad

3. Mad

4. Embarrassed

5. Guilty

There can be a variety of reasons that we do not make the best choices. Many of them fall into the following categories:

- Trying to Please Others

- Focusing on the Short-Term

- Using Our Hearts Instead of Our Heads

- Basing Decisions on Expectations of What We Think We "Deserve"

trying to please others

We all want to be liked. A lot of times, we tend to judge how wonderful we are by what others think about us. We decide that others must think we are great and show us a lot of attention in order for us to feel great. It often doesn't matter if the attention is positive or negative.

Can you think of a time when you or someone you know did something "just to get people talking"? Or a time when someone commented or "liked" their status on Facebook, Instagram, or other social media to stir up conversation? True, many of us will say we do not care what others think, or we tell ourselves to "shake those haters off". Yet, deep down inside, we want people to pay attention to us. We want them to care about us, and be with us. Often we will base our decisions on what we *think* will make us more likable to others. We believe that we will get invited to the best parties if we are more "fun" (such as being the one who drinks, breaks curfew, etc) so, we might make the choice to do those things to be with "The Party Crew". Other times, we may choose to get far more deeply involved in a dating relationship with someone than we are really ready for. We might have the fear that he or she will leave us if we do not "take it to the next level". The biggest emotion associated with making many of these bad choices is often fear. The fear of being abandoned or not liked can be overwhelming.

Has there ever been a time when you did something that you knew was not quite right, but you made the choice to do it anyway? If so, write about it here:

My "Trying to Please Others" Moment

_____

_____

_____

_____

_____

_____

_____

_____

Now, think about what you feared at that time? What made the choice a bad one? Looking back, what is it that you can say you learned from that moment?

Sometimes, in our pursuit of "Trying to Please Others" the person who is often left dissatisfied is…..ourselves. A person that would allow us to put our own wants and needs to the side for them obviously do not consider us a priority in their lives.

Have you ever made someone a priority (the most important person in your life) and he or she did the same for you? We usually want from others what they do not want or cannot give to us. It is important to learn to recognize when "Trying to Please Others", that the "others" are also out for our best interest as well.

how to tell if you are a priority or if they have your best interest at heart

1. When you are about to agree to do something that goes against the personal beliefs and/or values you have been taught, the person:

    a. Tells you to stop being "so good" and "have fun"

    b. Tells you they understand and suggest something else that goes along with your values

    c. Tell you it is ok, and then stops hanging with you

2. When you voice concern about engaging in a behavior that you are not ready for, the person:

    a. Reminds you that, if you cared about them, you would do it anyway

b. Will let you know that your opinion is valuable and you should not do anything you don't want to do

c. Tells you that you don't have to do anything you don't want to do, but they need to move on and find some-one who will

If the answers are anything but "B", you must begin to see that, "Trying to Please *Them*" may result in you making a decision that is not good for *you*.

focusing on the short-term

As a teen or "tween", it is difficult to imagine your life when you be-come 20, 30, or even 40. We may be able to say that "when I grow up, I want…." or "I want to be….", but how we get there is not always something we focus on. We may have a desire to become a teacher, but we do not realize that in order to become one we need to:

1. Get good grades in high school

2. Apply for money to attend school

3. Apply for colleges

4. Make sure to take classes in the subject I want to teach

We just know that we want to become *something*. What do you want to be when you grow up? Some of us have more than one idea. Take a second and pick only one. Have you thought about *all* of the steps you have to take to get there? The steps to achieve your goal are nothing more than a whole bunch of decisions that we have made over time.

It is easy to get caught up in what is happening right at this moment, or just what will happen this weekend. At times, that is an okay thing to do. Who wouldn't want to think about when their favorite musical artist is putting out their latest music or what they are going to do for their birthday? Even more importantly, wouldn't you want to know what you will GET for your birthday?

When our decisions focus only on "right now", we run the risk of doing something that can cause problems later. I like to call this the "It Feels Good Right Now" problem. This means that, we see only the short-term benefit of a choice we made.

We know we will get something we want right away from this choice. Yet, "It Feels Good Right Now" isn't the same as "Good for Me". Here's a simple example. Eating a whole bunch of pizza, ice cream, soda, chips, and cookies feels really good when you are eating them, however; it may make your stomach hurt later. Staying out all night with your friends may be fun as you hit up all the best parties, yet it may result in you getting grounded later.

Living in the "short-term" instead of thinking about the "long-term" means you might not think about the overall consequences of your choices. When thinking only the "short-term" we often fail to see that there may be very serious consequences for our choice. Let's go back and look at the "Eating a Whole Bunch of Stuff" situation. What could be some of the consequences that you may experience the next day or days after if you continue to eat like that? How about staying out all night with friends? What are the possible consequences for that?

choices

Now, it is your turn again. Think about one of your "Focusing on the Short-Term" times. Write about it here:

_____

_____

_____

_____

_____

_____

_____

_____

_____

_____

Let's look at the situation. What was the reason you chose to "Focus on the Short-term"? Here are some possibilities

1. It was something fun I wanted to do.

2. I didn't really think about anything but the moment.

3. I felt pressured by others

4. I thought of only the benefits and not the possible consequences

Name a couple of other possibilities here:

1. _____

2. _____

Due to the fact that this was one of the "not-so-good" decisions that you made, something negative that you did not like happened. The consequence may have occurred immediately, such as being grounded when you stayed out all night for a party, or could have been more long-term, such as being viewed as "the one your parents do not trust" because you chose to stay out all night. What happened because of your decision?

There is an old saying that "Hindsight is 20/20", which means, if we had the chance to go back, we would have made a different decision because we would know the consequence of the bad one. Let's do that with this choice. What other choice or choices would you make if you could go back and change the "Focusing on the Short-term" situation? *Don't forget to put what could have happened better or differently if you had made that other choice.*

_____

_____

_____

_____

_____

_____

Ask yourself these questions to begin to learn how to make better choices that look beyond the "short-term":What are the good things and bad things about making this decision?

1. How could this decision affect my relationship with others and how I think of myself?

2. What is the worst thing that could happen if I made this decision?

3. If this choice is about friendships, how will this improve my friendships? If it is about dating, what do I hope I will get from making this choice and what happens if it does not go the way I want it? Will I regret it later? If it is about rules, assuming I got caught, what could happen if I broke the rule?

4. Does this help get me closer to the goals that I have set for my life?

made with our hearts instead of our heads

Feelings are a very strong thing. It is because of our feelings that we laugh, cry, dance or just want to be alone. Our feelings determine a lot of our actions. Yet, we must not let our feelings alone make our choices for us. You may be known as a "Feeler" versus a "Thinker" when making decisions. No one is saying that it is a problem to "feel; however, you also need to put some "thought" into what you choose if you hope to make better decisions.

Are you a Thinker or a Feeler? (www.changingminds.org)

thinkers

+ Make decisions based primarily on what makes sense and when they do so, they consider a decision to be made.

+ Tend to see the world in black and white or Right vs. Wrong. There is no in-between

+ They think people are too wishy-washy and different, so they focus on things that do not change, look for the truth, and use clear rules.

+ At school, they are focused on completing tasks and schoolwork

+ Feelers may think you are cold or heartless

feelers

+ Make decisions based on how it will affect their relationships

+ Listen to their hearts

- Make decisions considering how it will make others feel

- Want to get along with others. They just want peace

- Choices are made based upon what is important to them (e.g. money, friendships, religious beliefs, etc)

- Thinkers may say you are "too emotional" and they cannot count on you

Just like in life, you must balance how you feel and think when making decisions. It is usually the "strong" feelings that make us forget to "think". Such as when you are:

- Excited

- "In Love"

- Scared

- Mad or Angry

- Depressed

Have you ever made decisions that you did not "think through" when having any of the above feelings? When you cleared your head and/or heart, did you begin to see things differently? When you find yourself in a situation that requires you to make a choice and you are experiencing *any* of these feelings, take a step back and BREATHE. Take time to THINK *before* you decide

choices based on expectations or what we think we "deserve"

As much as we would like to, no one grows up in a Fairytale. That is why they are fantasies. Stories that have been woven together with great imagination and shared with others. Your life experience may have been better or worse than others whom you may know. Regardless, better or worse, since it is *your* life, it is the only life that matters most to you. Our life situations may be considered "good", "okay", "bad", or even "horrible". Unfortunately, it is not uncommon for people to expect the same of us that they have seen in our family members. If your grandmother and mother were both teenage moms, do not be surprised if those around you "expect" the same of you. If your family is known for fighting, others might assume that you enjoy fighting as well.

Although such assumptions are not fair, they happen a lot more than we would like them to. The problem worsens when you start believing these same "bad expectations" about yourself. When we believe that we are "destined" to do wrong, or that we do not have potential, that is when we begin to make bad decisions.

Is your family "okay", "bad", or "horrible"? Think about what makes you believe this about them? Did someone say this was the type of family you had? Or did you make this judgment from your own experience and perceptions?

Have you ever been told that "You know…you are just like….." followed by something negative being said about you? Have you ever found yourself believing it? Why? When we believe other's bad expectations, we run into this:

believing bad expectations=
making bad choices

It is very important that you challenge the expectation that you are not capable, valuable, and WORTHY. We will discuss this in greater detail in a later chapter.

choices, choices

We have spent this chapter talking about "Choices" and how we make them every day. Even if this book was given to you, *you* made the choice to open the cover and read it. I hope that you also took the time to do the activities that are within it. Let's continue to take a look at some of the things that goes on in your life. We want to make sure that you get a clear understanding of how you can learn to make better decisions and become who you deserve to be.

affirmation

Every day, I make choices. I know that I have the ability to make good ones. I will remember that I am wonderfully-made and need to make decisions that will help me live to my fullest potential.

my thoughts on choices

_____

_____

_____

_____

_____

_____

_____

_____

_____

_____

_____

_____

_____

_____

you are worthy

"I'm not worthy" is a well-known saying. Do you know what that means? Not being worthy means that you are not deserving of the great things that are happening to you. When we do not expect that good things will happen to us or for us, we have accepted that our life will *always* be bad. We might even believe that we should accept when others do not treat us well, since "It Is What It Is."

Let's look at what "Worthy" means

- Valuable-*this means that you are worth something. That you are like none other and are uniquely great.*

- Deserving-*the best should happen to you. Nothing less is acceptable.*

- Honorable-*being of good character, honest, and fair.*

- Entitled to be respected-*No one should look down on you. No one should talk badly about you.*

Many girls do not feel worthy. They do not feel as if they should be treated well or that they should demand to be respected. Think about a time when someone disrespected you and you did not say anything about it. Write about it here:

_____

_____

_____

_____

_____

_____

How did you feel when this situation happened? Sometimes, we do not say anything because we believe that what occurred was our fault or that we ought to be treated that way.

Girls are not born thinking that they are unworthy; instead, it is something we learn. Usually, we learn it from those who are closest to us or from things surrounding us.

Some of the places where we learn our worth, or lack of it, are:

- Family

- "Friends"

- Music

- Television

- Books

Think about your family. Now, think about those members of your family who often make you feel good about yourself.

My Family Members Who Make Me Feel Good and Let Me Know I Am Worthy

_____

_____

_____

_____

_____

_____

What are some of the things these family members say to you that makes you feel good about yourself? Unfortunately, sometimes our own family members can be the ones in our lives to make us feel really bad about ourselves. It may not always be in the words that they actually say to us, or even in those things that they do not say.

here are some ways our family can make us feel badly about ourselves.

- You think you are better.....”
  If your family is doing well, others will try to make you feel bad about it. You might even downplay your worth. Even if your goal is not to "think you are better", others will try to transfer their own doubts and fears about themselves onto you. They will try to compare themselves to you and will try their best to make you feel ashamed of the good that is in you. What they don't understand is that it is not necessarily about being better. You just might be making better choices then they are----and there is *no* shame in that!

  Niya, 15 worked very hard in school. She had dreams of becoming a teacher, just like her favorite teacher Mrs. Johnson. Even when her cousins would try to get her to skip school and hang out, she would tell them that she couldn't because she had to get good grades if she wanted to go to college. One day when Niya again refused to skip school, her cousin India yelled at her "you just think you are better than everybody else. I can't stand bougie people!" Niya's feelings were hurt. She had never said anything bad about India and couldn't understand why her cousin would say such things.

- How a Parent's Behavior Can Affect How We Feel About Ourselves
  Some of us may have come from homes where our parents may not have made the best decisions. They may be

on drugs, in prison, have mental health problems, or just abandoned us. We may think that we could not be all that great since we were not worthy of our parents choosing to care for us over their own individual problems.

Sarah, 14 was raised by her grandmother after her mother went to prison for using drugs. Sarah never knew her father and felt embarrassed when people would talk about their own parents. Sarah thought that she was not worthy of respect or loved because her mother had chosen drugs over her. She was left to live with her grandmother. Sarah soon started hanging around with other kids that her grandmother didn't like. She figured the "good kids" wouldn't want to be bothered with someone who did not know her daddy and whose mom was in prison. Sarah believed that her mother's poor choices meant that she, herself, was a poor choice and not worthy of a good life.

◆ "Be Grateful"
Like Sarah, some of you are growing up without your parents. Instead you are living with grandparents, other relatives or even in foster care. You may have received messages from your caregivers that you are "lucky" that they will care for you or that you should "be grateful" that they are willing to do so. This can lead to you thinking that you are not special. It may make you feel that you are not deserving of support and love and that others only care for you out of charity because you do not deserve a good life.

Anika, 12 was in foster care after her parents got into trouble for neglecting to take care of her. At first, Anika was placed in the home with her two younger brothers, just as she did at home. Anika tried to look after her brothers, and would become upset when the foster parents would try and tell her how to raise them. Anika started to talk back to her foster mother after she heard her telephone conversation discussing how Anika should "be glad" that someone was willing to take her in their home after her own parents didn't want her.

◆ "You will be just like……"

As we discussed before, when individuals in your family make mistakes, others might automatically "predict" that you will also make the same poor decisions. They might tell you that "you will be just like….." or that you are just like your mom/dad/brother/sister….." When they make these statements you know that they are turning up their noses you. They do this due to the fact that they do not believe that your mom, dad, brother, or sister is a good person. When they say that you are like that person, they are letting you know that they believe that they see bad in you, or that you will make the same mistakes made by another member of your family. This narrow-minded and negative thinking does not allow you the freedom to be your own person and demonstrate your true value.

Although our parents' mistakes are their own, kids often have to live with the consequences of their parents' bad decisions and their problems. Just like Anika and Sarah, those around them had already decided that they would be a certain way because of decisions their parents had made. As unfair as this may seem, it is not unusual for family members, and others, who raise girls to make the mistake of thinking that this is true.

Has there ever been a time when someone in your family said or did something that made you feel bad about yourself? If so, what did they say?

_____

_____

_____

_____

_____

_____

Now, I want you to do something really hard. I want you to tell yourself that their negative statements are *NOT* true. Really think about what you would say and write it below. It may not be easy for you to know what to write. Ask someone who makes you feel good about yourself to help you out if you need to.

_____

_____

_____

_____

Our families don't just say things, they may also do things (or not do things) that can make us feel unworthy. Think about if any of the following situations have happened to you.

◆ They don't celebrate your achievements:
When you do well, people may act like it is not a big deal. You do not deserve the good grades, good friends, or making the sports team. This is not because you lack worth, but because others sometimes try to make themselves feel better by making you feel less about yourself

◆ You are a mistake:
They want you to accept that you are not worthy to try to make others' mistakes seem okay. Everyone is not raised in a family with both parents. Unfortunately, this sometimes means that out of anger a parent, grandparent or other family member may tell you that you were a mistake. This might be due to their belief that their decision to have you was not a good one for them.

The Bible talks about the fact that we are *all* gifts from God and that He does not make mistakes *(even if people do)*. Again, we may be made uncomfortable and not proud of who we are because others in our lives did not live up to *their* potential

23

All of the above are what we call "negative messages". This means that they are bad things that people say to us that make us feel lacking or unworthy. What are some of the other "negative messages" you have heard from family members?

_____

_____

_____

_____

_____

friends

Even though we discuss friends in a different chapter, we will talk about them briefly here.

How many of you WANT or like having friends? Everyone wants someone their own age that they can talk to and share things with. Yet, choosing the wrong friends can keep us from knowing our worth.

1. You want so badly to be liked that if someone else is not good at something, you will back off to prevent them from getting upset at you. You value their friendship more than following your own dreams. For example, you make the cheerleading squad or the volleyball team, but

quit because your friend did not make it---even though you always wanted to cheer or play sports.

2. Friends support each other. They do not compete with each other. I am not talking about good, old fashioned "healthy competition" such as "who can get better grades" or "who has on the nicest outfit". I am talking about that the kind of competing that is a direct result of envy and jealousy. It is all about wanting what you want or getting what you have.

Choosing the wrong friends can also make you feel unworthy. In the chapter on Friends, we will look at how to develop better friendships. In the meantime, write the names of the "friends" who have made you feel unworthy below. What have they done to you that has made you feel that way?: _____

facebook, instagram, books, songs, & television

People aren't the only ones who can make us think that we are not valuable or worthy. Everyday things that surround us, that we see and hear, can give us a false understanding of what girls of importance should be like. Think about your top 5 favorite songs that talk about girls or about being female. Write the names of the songs below:

_____

_____

_____

_____

_____

_____

Now, really think about the words to those songs. Listen very closely to the lyrics. What is the song saying about being a woman or a girl? Many times, music we listen to does not have the best message regarding young ladies or what others think are good qualities to find in girls. Instead, they might tell us that we should not like each other. They may tell us that we should do sexual and/or physical things that we are not ready for, or other demeaning things that are not good for us.. In listening to some of the more popular music, negative messages regarding girls might include:

> *Girls and/or women are not worthy of respect*-In some songs, the words that are used to describe young ladies are not very nice. Can you think of any of them? When we keep hearing ourselves called derogatory names, we may eventually start to believe that it is appropriate and start behaving like the name that we were called. Many of the names young ladies are called in songs are not ones that would make us feel worthy.

♦ *You are your bodies*- Songs may focus on your body or body parts. It might tell you how to "use" your body to prove your worth. Such messages may include that if you give "it" (your body) away someone will like you.

♦ *You are only good for non-committed relationships*-It is not about being married to someone and making a commitment in front of God---but instead just about giving yourself to someone briefly.

Do you like reality TV shows? They are everywhere now. Can you name a few of your favorite ones? How about regular TV shows that have girls and/or women in them? What are some of the things that have been said about females on these types of shows?

* *We are not expected to respect each other*-In many of the shows with girls or women, we are shown that we are supposed to talk bad about each other. Instead of being able to lean on each other for support, many television shows focus on girls hurting each other.

* *We are not worthy of respect by those in our lives*---we also learn that it is okay for others to talk about us or treat us wrong. In many of the reality shows, the females in them are cheated on, talked about, or otherwise disrespected. In the end, they return to relationships that are not healthy for them or worthy of them.

* *"Drama" needs to happen*-Let's be honest. No one watches reality shows for the "nice" or "polite" people. We quickly learn that, the more negative the attention you get, the more valued you are. Unfortunately, you get this attention by doing dumb stuff and /or making bad choices. This is also true in social media. You are likely to get more twitter followers, "friends on Facebook", or "hits on Instagram" when you say negative things about others or make comments that could be looked upon as threatening to others. Many of us also know of "that girl" who often posts

pictures of herself online that are showing her breasts, licking her lips, or showing her behind. We also see that these girls are the same ones that get the most comments from people around her....and we all like attention, right? We must really think about what type of attention we are worthy of receiving, and refuse to not settle for anything less.

instagram, facebook, snapchat,

Do you have a social media page or do you like to look at them? It would not be surprising if you did. You are growing up with technology that offers a variety of new ways to express yourself, connect, and stay in touch with people around you. Instagram, Facebook, Vine, and Snapchat offer you the chance to let the world get to opportunity to know you. Yet, they also make some girls think that they can "become whomever they want to be" without consequences. Are there some things you have seen people put on social media that makes you go "hmmmmm....oh....no she didn't?!" Write about them here:

_____

_____

_____

_____

_____

_____

Have you ever put something on your social media page that you wished you hadn't later? Why did you put it there in the first place? What made you realize that it probably wasn't a good idea? As we discussed in previous sections, we all want to be liked. We all like to have attention. The world of social media allows us to get attention from more people than we ever could in real day-to-day lives.

When we add up all of our "friends" and "followers" we begin to think that the more "friends" we have on social media, the more "likes" we will get for our pictures and messages. We feel that this says something about how popular or great a person we are. Our worth becomes based not on who we really are. Instead, we get wrapped up in a fake persona that we have created with posts that would make our grandma blush. We often use social media to send out the following messages about our worth:

- *I need to show my body*-we all know *that* girl who got 2,000 Facebook "likes" or 1500 Instagram "shares" because of showing her breasts, bending over and showing her behind, etc. Yet, we don't even care to look at the quality of a comment, but just that someone is saying *something* about us.

- *Cursing is the way to get my point across*---it has become comfortable to feel that, the more curse words we use in our posts, the more powerful they become. We may also think that such ways of talking make us appear cool. Yet, we fail to realize that the people who we are trying to impress with such language are not the ones worthy of impressing.

29

so, what can we do to help us recognize our worth?

- Self-evaluation-Sometimes, we really need to take a good look at ourselves, without hearing all of the negative messages around us. A good way to start this is by coming up with all of the great things that you feel you know about yourself. Try it now. Write a list of at least 5 good things about yourself here:

_____

_____

_____

_____

_____

_____

It might be easier to come up with the negative things about yourself, since we hear them more often. Still hold on to the list of the positives that we did earlier, and we will try to build on them later.

- Family
  Not all family members are bad. There are probably at least 1 or 2 people that you consider family who are consistently letting you know how great you are, or the potential you have to be wonderful. Begin listening to them. They are

likely the same people that you listed earlier in this chapter as those who are often supportive of you.

◆   Our True Friends
In the chapter on Friendships, we will take a look at what makes a *true* friend. However, for this chapter, we will just say to try to surround yourselves with people who meet the definition of good friends to help you feel good about yourself.

◆   Our Faith
Some people, (not all) have a religious belief or Higher Power to whom they look to for support. Most will say that their faith and/or Higher Power helps them and/or loves them. We can often find our worth through faith.

about me (fill in the blanks)

I am good at

_____

A positive thing about me is

_____

My future is bright because

_____

Something great I have to offer other people is

_____

When I grow up, I will become

_____

I deserve this from others

_____

affirmation

*I am deserving of all that is out here for me. I am valuable and will not let others tell me that I am not. I am intelligent, capable, and require respect. Those who disrespect me do not accept my worth and therefore are not worthy of my time. I will continue to strive to be the best that I can be---because I know that nothing less is ok. I am blessed and will be a blessing to others, because **I love me some me** and I AM WORTHY!*

my thoughts on my worth

_____

_____

_____

_____

_____

_____

_____

_____

_____

_____

_____

_____

_____

_____

friends, "frenemies", and others

We all want friends. We all want to like people and we want to be liked in return. Being in relationships with others seems to make sense and it is extremely important for all of us. What exactly do you think makes something a relationship?

Relationship Defined:

- Interaction between two or more people that have a significant impact on your life, behavior, emotions, and decision-making

Basically, a relationship involves you and at least one other person. In a relationship, you and the other person are likely to help each regarding decision-making, and determine what is and is not right. How you are able to get along with each other is likely to have a great impact on how you feel. There are many different types of relationships. All of them are not necessarily good for you. In this chapter, we are going to focus on defining friendships.

Friendships can be considered either healthy or unhealthy. When you think of a healthy relationship, write what you think it might include here:

_____

_____

_____

_____

_____

_____

As with anything else that we would consider "healthy", a "healthy" friendship is one that is good for you. It will make you feel good about yourself. It will actually be good for you. In a healthy friendship, the other person is very likely to encourage you to be the very best that you can be. They will support you when you make good decisions and won't hesitate to acknowledge the good that they see in you. Do you have a healthy friendship? If so, write about it here:

_____

_____

_____

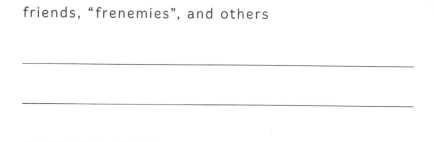

Sometimes, in our friendships, we just want the other person to agree with us. We want them to tell us we are good, even when we are not being good. We want them to tell us we are right, even when we are wrong. In a truly healthy friendship, honesty is a key part. Our "healthy" friends will tell us the truth, even if it is hard for us to hear. Yet, our true friends do not do this to be hurtful, it is told to us in a way that shows genuine concern and empathy. Have you ever had a friend tell you something that you knew was true, but you did not want to hear? How did you handle it? Why was it so difficult for you to hear it?

No one likes to have their bad behavior or any of their various problems pointed out to them. We also need to consider the person who is making the comments to us and try to understand what their true intention is toward us. Intention can also be known as the reason for something. Why is this person telling us this? When we look at a relationship as being healthy, the intention of a true friend pointing out negative things should be purely to make us a better person or to help us make better decisions.

Let's now look at unhealthy friendships. Have you ever been in one? What do you think makes a friendship unhealthy? Write your thoughts below:

_____

_____

_____

_____

_____

_____

_____

"Frenemies" is one term used to describe such friendships. What are other terms that you have heard?

_____

_____

_____

_____

_____

_____

Sometimes, we call friendships that are unhealthy "Toxic". Do you know what toxic means?

Toxic is often used as another word for poisonous. It probably won't kill you in small doses, however; in large doses things that are toxic can be deadly. How long can you be around a "toxic" person and survive? In a "toxic" friendship you may often be uncomfortable, disappointed, or have your feelings hurt, but it might not be "toxic" enough to make you call the friendship quits.

Kameron had known Antoinette since kindergarten. They lived on the same street and went to the same school. Things seem to go well until they got to middle school. Kameron started to notice that Antoinette would crack jokes about her to other girls. She would have sleepovers and make sure that Kameron knew about them, but wouldn't invite her. Kameron would tell Antoinette how her feelings were hurt. Antoinette would apologize, but would then go right back to cracking jokes at Kameron's expense and leaving her out of activities.

Exposure to toxic friendships over time can wreak havoc on a person. It is not healthy to be around someone who constantly puts you down, hurts your feelings, violates your trust or makes you doubt the good that is within you. Since this person does not truly care about what is really in your best interest, he or she will often pressure you to make decisions and/or do things that go against what you know is right. They may lead you to make decisions that leave you feeling ashamed or guilty. This can lead to a negative self-image and ruin the view you have of yourself.

Let's look at some examples of Toxic Friendships

the toxic friendship quiz

A. Instead of congratulating you on your successes, this friend does one or more of these:

1. Downplays it as not a big deal. For example "sure, your grades improved, but it's not like you got Straight As"

2. Insists upon one-upping you. For example "glad you got a new cellphone, but I'm buying a _____(fill in the blank with anything more expensive or "better" than yours)."

3. They just can't be happy for you. For example, "so? Who cares about_____(fill in the blank with your accomplishment)?

B. Discourages you from pursuing your dream:

1. Tells you that you are not strong enough, smart enough, or pretty enough to do something you have already set your mind to do. I am not talking about the TV talent show reject stuff when a person really cannot sing. Instead, this is when you have the ability or talent that you can do something with, and your so-called friend tries to keep you from doing it. They do not want you to succeed.

C. Instead of being supportive of you, they always seem to be in competition with you:

1. Whenever you try to do something, this person seeks out the same job, award, position, etc that you do. They are not necessarily interested in the sport, class, friend, or part in the play. They just do not want to see *you* get it. Sometimes, they just want to be able to let you see that he or she is "better" at something than you.

D. Talk about you like a dog to other people:

   1. This person makes it a priority to try to point out every negative thing about you that they can to others, regardless of whether they are true or not.

   2. They may always seem to know the latest "negative gossip" about you. They *swear* that others just "happen" to tell them these bad things. Think about it, why would someone feel completely comfortable telling your "friend" a lot of negative things about you? Only someone who believes that your so-called "friend" is okay with hearing negative things about you and willing to spread them to others.

If you agreed to any of these statements, then you must begin to realize that this person may not be your true friend. Can you think of other examples in your life of people who have not been your true friend? What led you to believe this? How did you stop the "friendship"? If you haven't stopped it, then what keeps you in it?

_____

_____

_____

_____

Another favorite statement is "I have no female friends". Have you ever said this yourself or heard other girls say it? Why do you think that girls have so many problems being friends with other girls? We hardly ever hear boys or men say they do not have any male friends. Let's look at some of the reasons why girls and/or women have so many problems being friends with each other. Finish this statement "Girls are......":

1. _____

2. _____

3. _____

4. _____

5. _____

What are some of the negative reasons girls give as to why they are not friends with other girls? If you haven't already said them, here might be a few that you have heard. Girls are: (1) petty (2) fake (3) talk about you behind your back, or (4) don't want the best for you. Did any of these reasons make your list? If there are other ones that you had not thought of, would you agree? Have you thought these same thoughts or said them before? Many times, our beliefs come from life experiences. Have you ever had a bad experience with another young lady that helped you to come up with these negative beliefs about females? Write about it here:

_____

_____

_____

_____

_____

_____

What have you learned about young ladies in the past that has negatively affected your desire to be friends with girls, or your willingness to trust them?

_____

_____

_____

_____

_____

_____

Here's a challenge for you. Have you had a bad experience in a friendship and/or relationship with a boy?

Write about it here: *If you have not had one personally, then write about one you know a friend has had:*

_____

_____

_____

_____

_____

_____

How has that negative experience influenced your perception of young men? Do you find that you do not want to be friends with boys or date them because of that bad experience? That is usually not the case. Often, we are a lot harder on ourselves and other young ladies than we are on young men. Why is that? We are more willing to look at a negative experience or situation with a boy or man as just one minor incident, however; we will *permanently* define another female by just one negative experience.

How can thinking bad thoughts about all other females keep you from the opportunity of some really great friendships?

Believe it or not, often *we* may not the best friends that we could be. Think about some of the toxic and/or unhealthy relationships that we discussed earlier in this chapter. Have *you* ever been that person? We may not have the best friendships due to the fact that what we are "putting out there" is not good. Have you ever heard of the expression, "Like Attracts Like"? Are you someone who truly cares about others? Are you someone who wants what is best for others and does not look to share their private "business" with others?

You might want to first take a look at yourself to see if you are the type of friend that you would want. How will you get friends if you aren't even the type of person that you would choose for friendship? What are some great things that you bring to a friendship? Take time to really think about it:

1. _____

2. _____

3. _____

4. _____

What are some things you might need to "work on" to be a better friend? Be honest with yourself.

1. _____

2. _____

3. _____

Sonia Jackson Myles, Founder, President & CEO of The Sister Accord, LLC said it best:

Friendship: What's Love Got To Do With It? The answer is everything. In order to be able to have healthy, positive interactions and relationships with other people, you must first be a friend to yourself. You must first love yourself. Once you are comfortable in your own skin, you can then see other people as an extension of yourself and your desire to ensure that your encounters are effective will be top of mind! The quality of your friendships are directly related to how you treat yourself. When you give your best, expect it in return. If there is no reciprocation of love respect, and support, it is time to reasses who is in your friendship circle.

going beyond toxic to bullying

There are relationships that don't seem to have any good in them. We had discussed Kameron's story earlier. At times it appeared that her friend Antoinette would be her "friend" when she felt like it. This made it hard Kameron to let the friendship go even though it was toxic. When we enter a relationship that is hurtful, scares us, makes us feel bad about ourselves, or appears to make us feel helpless, we have entered the area of bullying.

Many people make the mistake of thinking that bullying means a person has to punch or hit you. Believe it or not, some of the worst kind of bullying does not involve anything physical at all. According to www.stopbullying.gov, bullying includes actions such as making threats, spreading rumors, attacking someone physically or verbally, or purposely excluding someone from a group. Have you ever known of anyone who has been bullied? Write about it here:

_____

_____

_____

_____

_____

According to Carolyn Strong of Bullies Stink:

Bullying plain and simple is this, a situation in which one person is being picked on by another person and does not appear to be in a situation to defend themselves. Bullying can occur with one bully and one victim; it can occur with multiple bullies and multiple victims, or it can occur with multiple bullies and one victim; but the bottom line is this, whenever there is a bullying situation, you can rest assured that the person that is being bullied is being made to feel bad by the other person's behavior. And, in most cases, the person doing the bullying seems to be enjoying making the other person feel bad.

Again, there are many different types of bullying. Here is a more detailed explanation. Think about whether or not you have done any of these things or experienced them.

- **Verbal bullying** is saying or writing mean things. Verbal bullying includes:

  - Teasing

    - Calling someone names

    - Making inappropriate sexual comments to someone or about them

    - Threatening to harm someone

- **Social bullying**, sometimes referred to as relational bullying, involves hurting someone's reputation or relationships. This can include

  - Leaving someone out or not including them in social events on purpose

  - Telling other girls not to be friends with another

  - Spreading rumors about a person

  - Embarrassing someone in public

- **Physical bullying** involves hurting a person's body or possessions. Physical bullying includes:

  - Hitting, punching or slapping

  - Spitting

  - Tripping or pushing

  - Taking or breaking someone's things

A new form of bullying that has become increasingly popular with today's technology is called **Cyberbullying**

Cyberbullying takes place using electronic technology such as cellphones, computers, etc. It often takes place via text messages. It can also occur via social media sites such as Facebook, Instagram, etc. In cyberbullying, some of the same things we see in social and verbal bullying take place. For example

- Threatening to harm someone or calling them names via text messages or on Facebook

- Making up stories about the person and their reputation and posting it or texting it to others People can often say and do things that they would not do if the person was in front of them when they are involved in cyberbullying. Many times, cyberbullying can make girls feel even worse than verbal or social bullying. This is due to the fact that the bullying can spread further and involve more people due to the convenience of "sharing a status". People have the ability to "comment" on what was written which can sometimes lead to additional bullying. Thankfully, the law is finally catching up to technology. Cyberbullying is now considered a "criminal act". It can no longer be justified as just "fun".

Why do you think people bully?

_____

_____

_____

_____

_____

_____

Bullying is negative part of relationships that can cause us harm. It can make us feel bad about ourselves when we are bullied. Do you know of someone who has bullied others? Why do you think they choose to be a bully? What have you done when you have witnessed bullying?

Sometimes, people bully because they don't feel good about themselves. They see something in the other person that they wish that they possessed. How many of you have heard people say "She just thinks she's cute because.....?" Usually this is due to the fact that the person bullying might not like that particular piece of *herself* Instead of improving herself or learning to accept herself, she instead wants to make the other person hurt like she is hurting.

Think about someone you know who bullies others. What does she say or do? What do you think might be the reason that she bullies others? If you are that person who tends to act like a bully, why are some of the reasons that you think that you behave that way?

According to www.stopbullying.gov, some people are more likely to bully than others, including those who:

♦ Are aggressive or easily frustrated

♦ Have less parental involvement or are having issues at home

♦ Think badly of others

♦ Have difficulty following rules

♦ View violence in a positive way

♦ Have friends who bully others

Even if someone has a "reason" to bully, it is never okay to do so. Bullies like an audience and we have to make sure we that are not a part of it. What are some of the things you can do when you see someone being bullied?

_____

_____

_____

_____

_____

_____

Carolyn Strong of Bullies Stink reminds us:

If you witness bullying then there are several things that you can do. Confront the bully and tell them, "this is not something we do here" if you feel comfortable enough to do so. If you do not feel safe doing this, then know that no one expects you to. We do not want you to jeopardize your own safety, however; there are some other things that you can do.

- Find a trusted adult and report the behavior.

- Let a parent or guardian know so that they can tell someone who may be able to do something.

- Talk to the victim and let them know that they are not alone. Your words may be the only kind words that they hear that day. Kindness can make all the difference in the world for a victim of bullying.

Just as the victims of bullying need help, the bullies themselves need help to. We have got to work together to help end the cycle of hurt. That is the only way that we can begin the cycle of healing.

affirmation

I am valuable and must be respected in my relationships. I will settle for nothing less. I will work to be the kind of friend to others that I would want them to be for me.

my thoughts on my friendships

_____

_____

_____

_____

_____

_____

_____

_____

_____

_____

_____

_____

_____

_____

friends, "frenemies", and others

my thoughts on bullying

_____

_____

_____

_____

_____

_____

_____

_____

_____

_____

_____

_____

dating

What we learn about dating relationships, we usually learn from those around us. It does not necessarily take someone sitting down with us to talk to us about relationships for us to learn about them. Often, our first understanding of dating relationships comes from the adult women who have been entrusted with our care. The lessons we pick up from them may not always good ones, however; we get many ideas on relationships from them, anyway. Think about the adult female in your life who is most instrumental in raising you. What do you know about her dating or love relationship? Is it one that you would want for yourself? Why or why not? Think about other adult females in your life---grandmothers, aunts, foster mothers, stepmothers, mothers, etc. What have you learned about relationships from them? Let's take all of them into consideration and go in for a closer look:.

what they have taught me

What I have learned from the adult females in my life about:

Boys _____

_____

_____

_____

Dating _____

_____

_____

_____

Sex _____

_____

_____

_____

Marriage _____

_____

Do you feel that what you have learned is good, bad or a combination of both? Once again, what we learn is not about what is said, but more about what we see.

Tabitha, 14 is the oldest of her mother's 5 kids. Whenever her mother would start dating someone, she would get pregnant. Although her mother never said "you need to get pregnant to try and keep a man", Tabitha clearly seemed to learn this unspoken lesson from her mama.

Naomi, 12 saw her parents struggle to take care of her and her older sister. Her father and mother both worked hard to try and make sure that they had a roof over their heads. She would see her parents come home, both be exhausted, but each would help with homework, dinner, and then sit down with Naomi and her sister and ask about their day. Even though her parents did not say it, Naomi is learning that marriage is a partnership and you both try hard at making it work, even when it is hard.

Just because there is a message being learned about dating relationships, it does not mean you have to follow it. It is possible to "learn from someone else's mistakes" and work to have the opposite of the negative relationship that you have were witness to.. Are there some mistakes you have seen friends or family members make in dating relationships and marriages that have made you tell yourself that you will not make? What types of things made the relationship a mistake? What can you learn from it?

dating

_____

_____

_____

_____

_____

_____

There are other things that can teach us about dating. We can pick up messages from certain things that we watch on television, the music we listen to, and what we read. Let's take a closer look at those messages.

Think about your favorite television shows that have people on them who are dating or married. Write them here.

1. _____

2. _____

3. _____

What do each of those shows telling you about dating, marriage, or love?

_____

_____

_____

_____

_____

_____

Some messages seen in our television shows may include:

+ Relationships are among more than two people

+ Don't invest in one person, try dating several at a time

+ The more sexual you are, the more likely you are to "get the guy"

Do any of the shows you like have any of these messages? Do you believe them or see others in your life "live" the same way?

Let's look at the types of things that you read. I am not talking about the books that the adults in your life have picked out for you to read. We are talking about the types of books that you would choose to read for yourself. They may be books the adults in your life know you read, or then again.....maybe not.

Think about the most recent 3 books you chose to read. Or you can think about your favorite 3 books that have situations dealing with dating, marriage, or love relationships in them.

1. _____

2. _____

3. _____

What do feel each one of those books is telling you about dating, marriage, or love?

_____

_____

_____

_____

_____

_____

Some messages in books may include

- Seeking relationships for money—the goal of dating someone is to see how much they can give you or buy you

- Going outside of your own morals and values to "prove" your love even though you know the right thing to do, you will go against it in order to show the other person that you care

- Sex as a bargaining tool—you want the person to be in a relationship with you, so you either feel pressured to have sex or feel that, if you do, the person will love you or stay with you

Do any of the books you like have any of these messages? Do you believe them or see others in your life that "live" the same way?

Finally, let's take a look at some of the music you like. Keep in mind, this is about *you*, not what others want you to like. Think about your top 3 favorite songs that talk about dating, marriage, or love. Write them here:

1. _____

2. _____

3. _____

What do these songs tell you about dating, love, and marriage?

_____

_____

_____

_____

_____

_____

Messages in music

- Sexuality defines you as a female. The sexier you are, the more someone wants to be with you. You show your sexiness by the way you dress

- You must be willing to have sex in order for the relationship to work.

- You have to fight other females for your guy and it is not up to the guy to tell them to stay away.

Do any of the songs you like have any of these messages? Do you believe them or see others in your life that "live" the same way?

As you start moving towards the age of dating, let's examine why people even date. Write your reasons here.

1. _____

2. _____

3. _____

4. _____

5. _____

6. _____

Which of these reasons do you think are good ones?

If you decided to date, how would you know if your dating relationship was good or healthy for you?

Here is the Teen Dating Wheel. It takes a look at what a good dating relationship should include:

dating

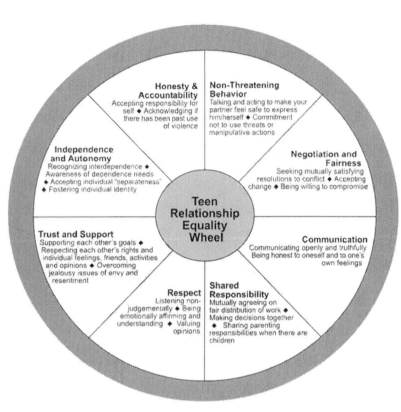

Wheel available at www.ncdsv.org
National Center on Domestic and Sexual Violence
Adapted from the *Power and Control Wheel* developed by Domestic Abuse
Intervention Programs, Duluth, MN.

Do you know of anyone who has had a healthy dating relationship? Have you ever had a healthy dating relationship? What feelings were associated with it?

_____

_____

_____

_____

_____

_____

_____

Unfortunately, not every dating relationship is good for you.

Just like friendships, dating relationships can be toxic. When you are in a toxic relationship, they may make you experience the following feelings:

- Emotionally drained

- Hopeless

- Tired

- Angry

dating

- Used

- Paranoid

- Stressed

- Resentful

When the relationship has moved from being toxic to becoming violent, you might get this dating wheel instead.

TEEN POWER AND CONTROL WHEEL

VIOLENCE

physical · sexual

PEER PRESSURE:
Threatening to expose someone's weakness or spread rumors. Telling malicious lies about an individual to peer group.

ANGER/EMOTIONAL ABUSE:
Putting her/him down. Making her/him feel bad about her or himself. Name calling. Making her/him think she/he's crazy. Playing mind games. Humiliating one another. Making her/him feel guilty.

ISOLATION/EXCLUSION:
Controlling what another does, who she/he sees and talks to, what she/he reads, where she/he goes. Limiting outside involvement. Using jealousy to justify actions

USING SOCIAL STATUS:
Treating her like a servant. Making all the decisions. Acting like the "master of the castle." Being the one to define men's and women's roles.

TEEN POWER AND CONTROL

SEXUAL COERCION:
Manipulating or making threats to get sex. Getting her pregnant. Threatening to take the children away. Getting someone drunk or drugged to get sex.

INTIMIDATION:
Making someone afraid by using looks, actions, gestures. Smashing things. Destroying property. Abusing pets. Displaying weapons.

THREATS:
Making and/or carrying out threats to do something to hurt another. Threatening to leave, to commit suicide, to report her/him to the police. Making her/him drop charges. Making her/him do illegal things.

MINIMIZE/DENY/BLAME:
Making light of the abuse and not taking concerns about it seriously. Saying the abuse didn't happen. Shifting responsibility for abusive behavior. Saying she/he caused it.

physical · sexual

VIOLENCE

Developed from:
Domestic Abuse Intervention Project
202 East Superior Street
Duluth, MN 55802
218.722.4134

Produced and distributed by:

NATIONAL CENTER
on Domestic and Sexual Violence
training · counseling · advocacy
7800 Shoal Creek, Ste 120-N · Austin, Texas 78757
tel: 512.407.9020 · fax: 512.407.9022 · www.ncdsv.org

Wheel available at www.ncdsv.org

dating

If a relationship is toxic or violent, why do we stay in them?

- *Thinking this is what love looks like*—sometimes, it is just because we do not know any better. It might be your first relationship, or from what you saw in adults around you, it might be what you have learned love is supposed to be

- *Low self-esteem/what you are worth*---this may be that the person you are dating tells you that you are the reason they act so bad, or you may have heard from family, friends, or others that you are not a good person. Hearing these negative messages, you might begin to believe that you deserve to be treated poorly.

- *Invested too much time*—no one likes to waste their time. If you have dated someone for awhile, you might think you have put too much time in that relationship to just "let go". As teenagers, 6 months of dating might seem like forever. Who are you to let 6 months of your life go down the drain by breaking up with him because he isn't always nice, talks badly about you, denies that you are dating, cheats on you, or even hits you once and awhile?

- *The other person will change*—have you ever thought "If I want it badly enough….."? We sometimes date people for who we want them to be, not who they really are. In doing so, we hope that, if we hang around long enough, he will become the person that cares about us.

- *It won't happen again*---this one is the most difficult. When bad things happen, we will tell ourselves that "he didn't mean it", "it won't happen again", etc. So we stay, in the hopes that, this will be the last time he (1) cheats (2) hits (3) acts like he doesn't know me.

- *If I love hard enough*---we may have seen those in our lives put up with a lot of mess and figure that, if we hold on and show the person how much we love him. If we remain that "ride or die chick", he will "come to his senses" and begin to see how special you are and treat you as such.

Have you ever stayed in a relationship for any of the reasons mentioned? Did you leave? If not, what continues to keep you there? Sometimes, it might be fear of what he will do to you if you go. You might have a fear for yourself that he will hurt you, or that he might even harm himself. If that is the case, it is important that you let an adult know immediately. Your relationship has gone from unhealthy to truly harmful for you. Some other places to get information when you are in a harmful relationship include:

dating

www.odvn.org

www.loveisrespect.org

www.loveisnotabuse.org

Affirmation

I was put on this earth to be loved and respected
Anyone who does not value all that I have to offer,
does not deserve me
I will seek relationships that are healthy and make me
feel good about myself
I will not let people stay in my life who do
not deserve to be there

my thoughts on dating

_____

_____

_____

_____

_____

_____

_____

_____

_____

_____

_____

_____

_____

you got this

Life is not always fair. No matter how much we want it to be, it is not. Can you think about a time when someone had more than enough "stuff"? You (or someone you know) barely had enough to even survive? Life is just not fair. Some of you may have had life experiences that no girl should ever have...and yet, you are still here.

There is something in you that has made it possible for you to continue to live life and strive for something better. Yes, sometimes life can remain unfair. You may wonder why your parents are not together when you see other people's parents happily married. You might question why your mother or father is incarcerated while other people's parents are able to go to work every day and most importantly, *come home.* You see your friend's dad picking her up from school and you get upset because you cannot understand why your dad chooses not to spend time with you.

Sigh... life is so unfair.

Yet, life is a journey and each person has their own. You did not originally choose to be on this path, but you can learn from it and begin to make decisions that will help you get to where you want to be. In order to do so, you must be open to exploring where you came from. You have to look within to see what you need to get where you want to be. Journeys are not always easy. The name itself sounds hard and long. I can just hear the theme music playing in the background. In your life's journey, you may initially start off in a place that is unfair. You might have time in your journey when you encounter others who may make it more difficult for you to continue. Yet, you choose to do it anyway.

What is there that you have experienced in the past that makes you feel that your life's journey has not always been fair? What are you currently experiencing that makes you feel that you are going through a tougher than usual journey?

_____

_____

_____

_____

_____

_____

These experiences can all be hurtful, scary, or sad for you. Believe it or not, negative experiences are an important part of discovering who you are and teaching you how to overcome obstacles. These experiences will strengthen you and allow you to prevent these past bad experiences from defining the rest of your life. Let's take a look at your journey thus far by using a house.

putting together your house

The foundation (bottom) of your house is your family and the good or bad experiences you have had with them. The foundation sets the stage for who we are, however; if the foundation is shaky or damaged we may struggle on how to build a better self from it. If your foundation was not or is not the best, add support beams that consist of the experiences and people you have had around you in your life that have made you stronger.

Next, we are going to look at the main part of the building. This is your positive and negative life experiences that have filled your space. The things that have helped or tried to hinder the process of you becoming the girl you are today. Everyone may not see these parts of you, but they do affect who you are and the solidity of your house.

Let's go to your windows. These are the way that people "see you". The windows are the way that you put yourself out there for the world to see. They might even include the way you look, activities you are in, or talents that you have.

The door to your home is next. We are going to leave it closed for the moment. Your door is what you need from others. This is how you invite others in to give you what you need. It might be love and acceptance. Unfortunately sometimes, it might be people who just "come in" to your home without invite and they may have brought you things that you do not need. These unwanted gifts can be hurt, pain or disappointment.

Let's look up at your roof. Your roof serves to "protect" your house. These are the skills and people you have that keep you going on your journey. They are the people and things you say to yourself that lets you know "I Got This". It helps you realize that you can do anything that you set your mind to.

Finally, there is a chimney. The chimney holds your dreams. It slowly let's them out so that they can actually occur. Add chimney smoke and write in it what you want for your life. In the actual chimney, write what you need to do to make those dreams come true.

my house

your journey

Again, life is sometimes unfair. Yet, being a young lady can be even more challenging. It is the time when we begin to figure out who you are and what you want. Your house may be your start, but it is only the first of many that you will "build". As you continue your journey, you will have the opportunity to tear down pieces, recognize others that do not fit, or try and start the entire construction project over. Part of looking at your life is asking yourself "Who Am I?" Have you ever done that before? Have you ever looked in the mirror and asked yourself that question? Let's do it now.

I AM.......

_____

_____

_____

_____

_____

_____

You might find that question difficult to answer. You might genuinely not be aware of who you are. You might start realizing things about yourself that may scare you or worry you. During this time, your body might be changing, and/or you might start seeing yourself

as "different" in some way from those around you. This may be due
to who you find yourself attracted to or what attracts your interest in
life. Yet, "different" does not have to equal "wrong"---instead, it can
be just another thing that makes you uniquely

YOU

What are some of the challenges you have faced as you try and
figure out you?

_____

_____

_____

_____

_____

_____

*Monica, 15 always felt "different". Even though she would joke about
dating with her friends, she never found herself attracted to boys. As
she sat down with her aunt, she broke in to tears and admitted that she
did not like boys and wanted to date girls.*

*Amy, 12 hated to change in the locker room for gym. She wanted noth-
ing more than to crawl in to the locker and hope that no one else could
see that she had not become "a woman" yet.*

In deciding who you are, it is important to identify friends and adults who are supportive of you and want nothing more than to help you on this journey of figuring out you.

After figuring out who you are, you then need to figure out who you want to be. How do you see yourself/your house in 5 years, 10 years?

I WANT TO BE......
_____

As you look at your journey, it is important that you recognize that you have the ability to be anything you want to be. You must begin to see the pieces of yourself that can help you achieve your goals. So, what is it about you that lets you know that "You got this?" What about you makes you the strong, wonderful person that you are and will be?

Write about what makes you uniquely, exceptionally you.

_____

_____

_____

_____

_____

_____

There are many women who were once girls like you. Just like you, they have experienced dating, choices, friendship problems, and growing up. Here are some words from some of them.

Sometimes unfortunate, unexpected, and unfair things happen to amazing people. You are still amazing. You are still gifted, talented, and full of potential. More importantly, you are not alone! You have sister-friends all across the world that stand behind you cheering you toward greatness! I am one of them! ---*Rev. R. Janae Pitts-Murdock, Southern Regional Chaplain, Delta Sigma Theta Sorority, Inc*

One of the most valuable lessons I have learned is that your mistakes can be your most valuable assets. To leverage your mistakes, here are some rules of thumb: First, you must act with integrity and determination in all things. Second, you must remain focused like a laser on your unique vision for success for your life. Third, and probably most importantly, you must *learn from the mistakes you make.* If you don't make mistakes, you're not taking enough risks, so be courageous! Fall. Bump your head and scrape your knee. The bumps and bruises make you wiser, stronger, and more resilient. Your task is to remember where the trip-points are you've already experienced so that you never trip on the same crack in the sidewalk again.---*Dr. Rachel Talton, CEO of Synergy Marketing Strategy & Research, Inc. and CTO of Flourish Leadership, LLC*

Girls--You are all part of the Divine Feminine. An energy created by God that will be taking its place in this age that will bring tremendous healing and balance to our Beautiful Mother Earth. Nurture your inner beauty and share your gifts with the world that needs each of you so greatly.---*Dr. Evelyn Rivera, Bilingual Psychologist*

You are worth it!. You are worth being listened to, cared for and loved. I am sorry no one listened to you when you tried to say that you were being hurt or mistreated. I am sorry no one cared enough to protect you or were too busy for you. You are worth the wait! Worth all the time and energy it takes to learn you are Beautiful and Important! You are worth it!--- *Antoinette Byrd-Carr, MD, MS Obstetrics & Gynecology Detroit, MI*

Visualize your future and make decisions everyday that will allow you to make that vision a reality.—*Dr. Satira Streeter, Executive Director, Ascensions Psychological Services*

DO YOU, BE YOU, BELIEVE IN YOURSELF! Don't compare your inside with someone's outside...---*Yvonne Hunnicutt, Child Welfare Advocate*

The best gift that you can give the world is to be your best self rather than a substandard copy of someone else. God made you who he wanted you to be; trust that he doesn't make mistakes.— *Carolyn Strong, Founder of Bullies Stink and author of* Black Girl Blues

You are more than your physical attributes. However, still accept them, love them, but never let anyone disrespect them or you. ----*Milvon Wright, Social Worker*

The cornerstone to everything is foundation and faith. If you ever aspire to be really successful train yourself to do the BIG stuff first. The greatest advantage of youth is having a fresh mind, a willing spirit and perseverance. The ingredients of a firm foundation, mixed with faith and youth, is an unfailing resource that will carry you strongly in adulthood----*Sherita Carthon, Motivational Speaker, Retail Maven*

You are far more valuable than the sum of your experiences. Every life lesson increases your worth. Every failure elevates your character. My words of wisdom, keep rising. ---*Rev. Renee L. Bradford, Founder/Vision Keeper, First Purse, Inc.*

You are at a critical phase in your life. You have some important decisions to make. The most important one being deciding who YOU will be. Either YOU can choose who you are going to be or...the people around you will decide for you. What do YOU choose?---*Dr. Karen Townsend, Www.AboutMySisters.com*

Think on this, you and all of creation are truly amazing. There is no one on earth exactly like *you* and that makes *you* special. Learn to love yourself, forgive yourself, speak up for yourself and be yourself. Everyday commit to being your best self. Patti Labelle said, "Remember, you don't need a certain number of friends, just a number of friends you can be certain of."--- *Becky Palmer, MS Trainer, Consultant & Therapist*

Now, find someone who is helping you in this journey and ask them to write some words of encouragement to you. Use these words of encouragement to look back on when life is feeling really unfair.

_____

_____

_____

_____

_____

_____

Affirmation

Life is not always fair
I cannot spend my time waiting for it to become fair
Instead, I will face the challenges that come my way
As I figure out who I am and who I want to become,
And build the "house" I deserve
Life is a journey and I am ready and able to go on it
Cause "I GOT THIS!"

my thoughts on me

_____

_____

_____

_____

_____

_____

_____

_____

_____

_____

_____

_____

my advice to other girls

_____

_____

_____

_____

_____

_____

_____

_____

_____

_____

_____

_____

_____

additional resources

www.bulliesstink.com
Offers resources for addressing bullying include link to <u>Black Girl Blues</u>, an activity book to combat intra-racial bullying

www.TheSisterAccord.com
Website addressing principles of sisterhood. Provides information on upcoming events supporting the concept of sisterhood in women and girls.

http://www.youngwomenshealth.org/PDFs/curric_healthy_relat.pdf
Provides a module of activities to better explore development of healthy relationships

http://www.vtnetwork.org/wp-content/uploads/Youth-Advocate-and-Educator-Activity-Manaual.pdf
Youth and Child Advocate and Educator Manual of Activities and Exercises for Children and Youth
Variety of topics including healthy relationships, icebreakers, feelings, and teamwork

http://idvsa.org/wp-content/uploads/2013/01/Parent-Middle-School-Student-Workshop.pdf
Start Strong Idaho: Building Healthy Teen Relationships Start Relating before They Start Dating: A Workshop for Parents and Caregivers, and their Teens

Curriculum for parents/caregivers and teens addressing healthy relationships

http://www.advocatesforyouth.org/storage/advfy/documents/chapter4.pdf
Life Planning Education, Advocates for Youth
Addresses family relationships and friendships

http://www.mentoring.org/downloads/mentoring_429.pdf
Baylor University's Community Mentoring for Adolescent Development
Addresses goal setting and decision-making

https://apps.state.or.us/Forms/Served/de0087.pdf
My future, My Choice curriculum by Oregon Department of Human Services, Children, Adults and Family Division
Curriculum on decision-making, choices, and sexual choices

about the author

Dr. Tyffani Monford Dent is a licensed psychologist/motivational speaker/author. She lectures and trains on issues of mental health disparity in minority communities, children's and women's issues, and sexual abuse intervention and prevention. Dr. Dent is also the Executive Director of Monford Dent Consulting & Psychological Services, LLC. She is the author of another book entitled <u>Girls Got Issues: A Woman's Guide to Self-discovery & Healing</u> available at various internet retailers and on her website www.MonfordDentConsulting.com. Follow her on twitter: drtyffanimdent

Made in the USA
Charleston, SC
18 October 2014